Peculiar Plants of the World

Plants That Eat Meat

Beatrice Loukopoulos

PowerKiDS press
New York

Published in 2019 by The Rosen Publishing Group, Inc.
29 East 21st Street, New York, NY 10010

Editor: Elizabeth Krajnik
Book Design: Rachel Rising

Photo Credits: Cover (Venus flytrap) Marco Uliana/Shutterstock.com; Cover (pitcher plant) cozyta/Shutterstock.com; Cover, pp. 1, 3, 4, 5, 6, 8, 9, 10, 12, 14,16, 18, 20, 21, 22, 23, 24 (background) Only background/Shutterstock.com; p. 4 Number One/Shutterstock.com; p. 5 Nattaphun.Tee/Shutterstock.com; p. 7 Vlue/Shutterstock.com; p. 8 ShutterOK/Shutterstock.com; p. 9 Cathy Keifer/Shutterstock.com; p. 11 Alexander_N/Shutterstock.com; p. 13 Oleksandra Petrovska/Shutterstock.com; p. 14 Mageon/Shutterstock.com; p. 15 Linas T/Shutterstock.com; p. 16, 17 mccw thissen/Shutterstock.com; p. 18 Luka Hercigonja/Shutterstock.com; p. 19 Jeff Holcombe/Shutterstock.com; p. 20 PHOTO FUN/Shutterstock.com; p. 21 Bart Achilles/Shutterstock.com; p. 22 Paul Starosta/Corbis Documentary/Getty Images.

Cataloging-in-Publication Data

Names: Loukopoulos, Beatrice.
Title: Plants that eat meat / Beatrice Loukopoulos.
Description: New York : PowerKids Press, 2020. | Series: Peculiar plants of the world | Includes glossary and index.
Identifiers: ISBN 9781538346020 (pbk.) | ISBN 9781538344903 (library bound) | ISBN 9781538346037 (6 pack)
Subjects: LCSH: Carnivorous plants–Juvenile literature.
Classification: LCC QK917.L68 2020 | DDC 583'.887–dc23

Manufactured in the United States of America

CPSIA Compliance Information. Batch #CWPK19. For Further Information contact Rosen Publishing, New York, New York at 1-800-237-9932

Contents

Meat-Eating Plants 4
Supporting Life 6
A Tasty Meal 8
Where Do Carnivorous Plants Grow? 10
Can I Grow Carnivorous Plants? 12
The Venus Flytrap 14
Pitcher Plants 16
Bladderworts 18
The Sundew 20
Other Carnivorous Plants 22
Glossary 23
Index 24
Websites 24

Meat-Eating Plants

Plants are all around us. They're in people's gardens, in their homes, and in greenhouses. What do you know about plants? Most plants don't get their food the way we do. You probably know that most plants need water, sunlight, and soil to make their own food and grow. However, not all plants get their food this way.

VENUS FLYTRAP

There are more than 600 species, or kinds, of carnivorous plants.

SUN PITCHER

Some plants have **adapted** to living in places where the soil doesn't give them enough **nutrients**. Some of these plants are **carnivorous**. They eat **insects** and other small animals to get the nutrients they need. There are different kinds of carnivorous plants. Let's learn about a few of them!

Supporting Life

Plants need food and water to live. They take in a gas called carbon dioxide from the air. With carbon dioxide, sunlight, and water, plants create their own food through a **process** called photosynthesis. Carnivorous plants can photosynthesize, but they need extra nutrients as well. Meat-eating plants have parts such as sharp or sticky hairs and slippery leaves to help them catch food.

All kinds of living things have to reproduce, or produce another living thing of the same kind, to help their species survive. Carnivorous plants reproduce in many ways. They can spread seeds or send out special shoots. Larger plants can also separate into many smaller plants.

Plant Particulars

Sometimes plants need help reproducing. Birds and other animals eat the plants' seeds. When the animals poop, the seeds have the chance to grow in a new place.

Plants with roots draw nutrients and water from the soil. However, sometimes plants don't get everything they need from the soil in their surroundings.

A Tasty Meal

Why are animals attracted to, or drawn toward, carnivorous plants? Some plants have sweet-smelling **nectar** while others collect rainwater that animals may want to drink.

Carnivorous plants don't have teeth, throats, or stomachs. So how do they eat animals? Most carnivorous plants make a **fluid** that digests, or breaks down, food just as our stomach **acid** does for us.

Some carnivorous plants, such as the sundew, trap their tasty meals using a flypaper trap, which is a trap covered with a sticky, glue-like **substance**.

Some meat-eating plants make **chemicals** that keep their prey, or the animals they use for food, from moving. Other meat-eating plants make **antibiotics** to keep bacteria from growing on their food while they're digesting it. It takes some plants almost two weeks to digest an insect.

Where Do Carnivorous Plants Grow?

Carnivorous plants grow on every **continent** on Earth except Antarctica. They grow in different places, including on mountainsides and in forests. However, most carnivorous plants have a type of **habitat** in common.

Carnivorous plants grow best in soil that is wet and acidic. All plants need **nitrogen** to live and grow. Watery soil has little nitrogen. The water carries it away. Luckily for carnivorous plants, there is plenty of nitrogen in the animals they eat. Many of these plants can live without eating meat. However, they grow better when they get nitrogen from animals.

Many carnivorous plants grow in or near bogs, which are areas of wet, spongy, acidic soil that are found next to a body of water, such as a pond.

Can I Grow Carnivorous Plants?

Many people grow carnivorous plants in their homes or in their gardens. However, not all of these plants grow well in certain areas. Someone living in a very dry area wouldn't be able to grow these plants in an outdoor garden.

Many carnivorous plants are endangered, or in danger of dying out. By growing these endangered plants in greenhouses, people are able to keep them from dying out. However, people's interest in carnivorous plants has caused problems, too. Some people take plants from the wild to grow them at home. This is one reason why so many of these plants are endangered.

Plant Particulars

Many species of carnivorous plants are on the endangered species list. In fact, around 27 species are listed as in trouble.

One way you can find out whether a carnivorous plant will grow where you live is to get in touch with a carnivorous plant club in your area. These people will know if the soil where you live is right for a carnivorous plant.

The Venus Flytrap

The Venus flytrap is one of the most well-known carnivorous plants. It's insectivorous, which means it eats insects. In the wild, it lives in only a few swampy places in North Carolina and South Carolina. It's also grown in greenhouses.

The Venus flytrap has special leaves that have two parts, or lobes. These lobes have fine hairs on them. If an insect touches these hairs as it lands on the leaf, the lobes snap together. Once a bug is trapped inside, the lobes secrete, or put out, digestive fluid. It can take the Venus flytrap up to 10 days to digest an insect. Then it opens up again.

Plant Particulars

Insects are attracted to the Venus flytrap because it secretes sweet-smelling nectar. The trap closes around the insect tightly after a few seconds.

The Venus flytrap has four fine hairs on the inside of each leaf. These hairs are called trigger hairs. A trigger is something that causes something else to happen.

Pitcher Plants

Pitcher plants, which get their name from their pitcher-shaped leaves, grow mainly in two parts of the world: along the eastern coast of the United States and Canada and in rain forests in Asia. The leaves of pitcher plants hold water just as a pitcher in your kitchen does.

How do pitcher plants trap their prey? Animals are attracted to a sweet nectar near the top of the pitcher-shaped leaves. These leaves act as a pitfall trap, which means the animals fall into the pit formed by the leaves. Bugs end up drowning in the pitcher's digestive fluid, which breaks down the insect's body.

Plant Particulars

Some species of pitcher plants have tiny hairs inside the leaves that point downward to trap their prey. Others have smooth leaves so the prey can't climb out.

Some pitcher plants are only about 4 inches (10.2 cm) tall. Others can grow as tall as 4 feet (1.2 m). Pitcher plants also come in many colors, including green, yellow, white, and red.

Bladderworts

Bladderworts are rootless carnivorous plants that grow on land under very wet soil or in water in ponds and swamps. The bladderwort's underground or underwater stems are covered in hundreds of clear bags called bladders. Bladderworts trap the small insects and other animals they eat in the bladders.

The bladderwort's bladder traps are a kind of special leaf connected to the plant's stem. Each trap has a door that only opens inward. When prey touches one of the trigger hairs near the trapdoor, the door opens and water and the insect are sucked inside the bladder. This type of trap is called a suction trap.

Plant Particulars

The bladderwort can digest its prey within 15 minutes. Then the trap is ready for another insect or small animal to trigger the trapdoor.

The bladderwort's traps can be as small as a pinhead to as large as one-eighth of an inch (0.32 cm) wide.

The Sundew

The sundew is a carnivorous plant that grows in many places around the world. The leaves of the sundew have hairlike structures that have drops of sticky liquid at the tip. The drops act like glue to trap the plant's prey, almost like a spiderweb.

Each sundew leaf has about 250 hairs on it. These hairs are often called tentacles, which are long, movable arms on a plant or animal.

Once the plant traps its prey, the hairlike structures begin to curl around the insect. When the insect tries to get away, the hairs wrap around it even tighter to keep it there. Soon the bug can't breathe and dies. At the base of the hairlike structures, there's a part of the plant that makes digestive fluid with which to eat the insect.

Other Carnivorous Plants

Carnivorous plants grow all around the world. Butterworts, which grow throughout the southwestern United States, use a sticky glue-like substance on the tip of their hairlike structures to trap their prey. This plant may have gotten its name because its leaves look kind of shiny—almost like butter—and can be a soft greenish-yellow color.

Another type of carnivorous plant is the dewy pine. This plant grows in the wild in Portugal, Spain, and Morocco and grows well in areas with warm, wet winters and hot, dry summers. Dewy pines have yellow flowers and give off a honey smell to attract prey.

BUTTERWORT

Glossary

adapt: To change to suit conditions.

acid: A liquid that breaks down matter.

antibiotic: A drug that can kill germs, including harmful bacteria.

carnivorous: Feeding on animal flesh or tissue.

chemical: Matter that can be mixed with other matter to cause changes.

continent: One of the great separations of land on Earth—Africa, Antarctica, Asia, Australia, Europe, North America, and South America.

fluid: A substance that flows freely like water.

habitat: The natural home for plants, animals, and other living things.

insect: A small animal that has six legs and a body formed of three parts and that may have wings.

nectar: A sweet liquid produced by plants and used by bees in making honey.

nitrogen: A chemical with no taste or smell that makes up a large part of Earth's atmosphere and is present in all living things.

nutrient: Something taken in by a plant or animal that helps it grow and stay healthy.

process: A set of actions that produce something or that lead to a particular result.

substance: Matter of a certain kind.

Index

A
animals, 5, 6, 8, 9, 10, 16, 18
Antarctica, 10
Asia, 16

B
bladders, 18
bladderworts, 18, 19
butterwort, 22

C
Canada, 16
carbon dioxide, 6

D
dewy pine, 22

F
flypaper trap, 9

G
greenhouse, 4, 12, 14

H
hairs, 6, 14, 15, 16, 18, 21

I
insects, 5, 9, 14, 16, 18, 21

L
leaves, 6, 14, 15, 16, 18, 20, 21, 22

M
Morocco, 22

N
nectar, 8, 14, 16
nitrogen, 10
North Carolina, 14
nutrients, 5, 6, 7

P
pitcher plant, 5, 16, 17
pitfall trap, 16
Portugal, 22

S
seeds, 6
soil, 4, 5, 7, 10, 11, 13, 18
South Carolina, 14
Spain, 22
suction trap, 18
sundew, 9, 20, 21
sunlight, 4, 6
sun pitcher, 5

T
tentacles, 21

U
United States, 16, 22

V
Venus flytrap, 4, 14, 15

W
water, 4, 6, 7, 8, 10, 11, 16, 18

Websites

Due to the changing nature of Internet links, PowerKids Press has developed an online list of websites related to the subject of this book. This site is updated regularly. Please use this link to access the list:
www.powerkidslinks.com/ppw/meat